The Least

The Least

Poems

Mac Gay

Iris Press
Oak Ridge, Tennessee

Copyright © 2022 by Mac Gay

Cover Photograph and Book Design by Robert B. Cumming, Jr.

Library of Congress Cataloging-in-Publication Data

Names: Gay, Mac, author.
Title: The least : poems / Mac Gay.
Description: Oak Ridge, Tennessee : Iris Press, [2022] | Summary:
  "Ultimately, we all end up losers, at least to the atheist or agnostic,
  but The Least by Mac Gay documents a sample of the myriad that get a
  head start, whether as the unfortunate, the infamous, or the exhausted,
  for as Victor Hugo mentions concerning his voluminous tome Les
  Miserables, "there is a point... at which the unfortunate and the
  infamous are associated into a single word." And that word, his book's
  title, translates for this book's purposes into The Least. Gay's
  narratives and dramatic monologues describe individually and in detail
  the misfits and the misbegotten, the tired, the unlucky, and the
  antiheroic, in all their pain, misery, and frustration. Perhaps we are
  all frail, comic facsimiles of Jesus, stumbling along in the dark,
  falling into our various foibles, pitfalls, and vices, longing for
  redemption. Whether readers can find themselves here or not is for them
  to discover, but the author in some strange way finds himself on nearly
  every page. Let the believers be reminded of Jesus's declaration from
  the book of Mark: "Inasmuch as ye have done it unto one of the least of
  these my brethren ye have done it unto me.""— Provided by publisher.
Identifiers: LCCN 2022023288 (print) | LCCN 2022023289 (ebook) | ISBN
  9781604542660 (paperback) | ISBN 9781604548204 (ebook)
Subjects: LCGFT: Poetry.
Classification: LCC PS3607.A9856 L43 2022 (print) | LCC PS3607.A9856
  (ebook) | DDC 811/.6—dc23/eng/20220518
LC record available at https://lccn.loc.gov/2022023288
LC ebook record available at https://lccn.loc.gov/2022023289

Acknowledgments

Grateful acknowledgment is made to the editors of the following magazines in which these poems have appeared, some in slightly different form or with different titles:

Agnes Scott Writers Festival Magazine: "Advice"
Construction Literary Magazine: "Real Churches"
Crosswinds Literary Journal: "Old Jock at Sunny Shores," "Voice from the Window Bed" (finalist for the 2021 Crosswinds Poetry Prize selected by Margaret Gibson, Poet Laureate of Connecticut)
North of Oxford: "Closure"
Plainsong: "The Drowned Man"
Poems & Plays:" Poolroom"
Rat's Ass Review: "At Woodlawn," "Black Hole," "Hard Time," "On the Euthanasia of Dogs," and "Uncle Cried Uncle"
Red Rock Review: "Snakebit"
Snake Nation Review: "Guilt"
The American Journal of Poetry: "Demolition," "Estate Sale," "Harrowing," "Mrs. Sharkly's War," and "The Widow Recalls the Storm"
The Atlanta Review: "The Ladies" and "Murder House"
The Parliament Literary Journal: "The Catcher in the Wry" and "Killer"
The Raintown Review: "The Landlord Discusses Business with His Son" and "T-bone"

The following poems were included in *Farm Alarm* (runner up for Texas Review Press's 2018 Robert Phillips Poetry Chapbook Prize): "At Woodlawn," "Closure," "Cobbler," "Crap Shoot," "Hot Rod," and "Squirrel Creek Farm"

The following poem appeared in the 2017 chapbook *Pluto's Despair* from Kattywompus Press: "Poolroom"

The following poems appeared in the chapbook *Physical Science* (winner of the 2003 Tennessee Poetry Chapbook Prize) from *Poems & Plays*: "Cad," "Day's End," and "Subtraction"

And the King shall answer and say unto them, Verily I say unto you, Inasmuch as ye have done it unto one of the least of these my brethren, ye have it unto me.

—Matthew 25:40 KJV

…there is a point, moreover, at which the unfortunate and the infamous are associated and confounded into a single word…

—Victor Hugo *Les Miserables*

Contents

I THE UNFORTUNATE

Harrowing • 13
Hot Rod • 14
Closure • 15
Cowboy Death • 16
Black Hole • 17
Sublimation • 18
Crapshoot • 19
Venus and T • 21
T-bone • 22
Hard Head • 23
Uncle Rush Speaks • 24
Allie's Elegy • 25
Advice • 26
Home from Afghanistan • 27
Yardman • 28
Estate Sale • 29
On the Euthanasia of Dogs • 30
Snakebit • 31
The Drowned Man • 32
Uncle Cried Uncle • 33
Plague • 34
Ghosts • 35

II THE INFAMOUS

The Widow Recalls the Storm • 39
Poolroom • 40
Catcher in the Wry • 41
Real Churches • 42
Mrs. Sharkly's War • 43
Cad • 44
Demolition • 45
Day's End • 46
Jackoff of All Trades • 48
News Flash • 49
Like a Good Neighbor • 50
Guilt • 51
The Baby Speaks • 53
Sorcerer's Rope • 54
Mob • 55
Slow Learner • 56

Bad Boss Confidential • 57
Wednesday When I Called • 58
Murder House • 59
Anatomy Lesson • 60
Niches • 61
Squirrel Creek Farm • 62
Killer • 63
Mr. Cutter of the Sandtown Group • 64
The Landlord Discusses Business with His Son • 65
Boomer at the Birth of Jim Crow's Doom • 66
Pale William's Lament • 67
Pale William as a Boy • 68

III THE EXHAUSTED

Cobbler • 71
Voice from the Window Bed • 72
Old Jock at Sunny Shores • 74
The Ladies • 75
Ghost Hunter • 76
Our Dying Neighbor Cuts the Grass • 77
High Blood • 78
At Woodlawn • 79
Hard Time • 80
The Old Man and the Black Dog • 81
Mirror, Mirror • 82
Fourth Step • 83
Preserves • 84
Subtraction • 85

THE UNFORTUNATE

Harrowing

Maybe he was trying to amuse the boy,
or inculcate virtues of work: whatever
reason you'd give for inviting a child
to ride with you on the John Deere.
Said instruction might teach
how to plow a spring field,
fall in love with the smell
of fuel oil and newly-torn soil,
that breathtaking slicing of earth;
or the stout agricultural swirl
of getting work done that's
essential. Yet any old man can tell
you of days that slip out of joint
like a 9.0 monster earthquake
before you can say Jack Robinson,
as when a small boy slips off the back
in a sort of fantastical red-dusty blur
and under the discs of the bush and bog.
Our falling, our failing, is always nightmare,
whether plowing a field or believing
a blue sky can't kill. But a ton of a harrow
cuts through 6-year-old bone to reality's marrow.
Blood dries, turns black, rain washes away,
but how would you wash that sight out of your head?
Mr. Jones thought a 12 gauge might do it.
Before half a year, Mr. Samuel Jones proved it.

Hot Rod

James Hancock was not John, but when
James drove he too writ his name large.
Sophomore, a year ahead, he kindly chauffeured
me the twelve miles home some afternoons
after late August football drills. I recall well
his '59 baby blue, moon-hubbed Ford
growling loud and flying east down 36,
James passing cars left and right, no bull,
he did a thing I'd never seen—he passed
cars on the ditch-side of the road. I shit
you not, my friend, and not once hit a sign,
or slid off in the ditch. Son of a bitch!,
I mumbled to myself, me, who loved a thrill—
but it wasn't many weeks I heard the tale
which really made me suck my breath, all sick,
of James my wild-ass friend's decapitation
post rear-ending an Old Dominion semi-truck.
The news of James' grave miscalculation
brought shock, but no surprise.
Still, just sixteen, and dead.
And no way round the awful fact
that James' dense, impatient foot
proved swifter than his head.

Closure

That's what Dad always wanted.
"Close the door behind you," he'd snap,
or "Did you take out the trash?" The man
hated loose ends, any task dragging
from one day into the next. "You
finish your algebra?" he'd fling at me
blind from behind his newspaper.
Or "Let's finish trimming these hedges
before darkness takes us over."
(Nothing was worse than uneven
Red-tip Photinias.) But the thing
he hated most was getting old:
"Old men are like broken tools
or leaky buckets," he said,
"or the invisible man in the movies,
just fading and fading until he'd
have to wrap himself with rolls of gauze
just so folks would know he was still there."
So Mom took some comfort later
from his bad good luck. That
Sunday morning he left with Bo
to put a neck yoke on the crazy cow
that kept jumping over the fence.
He aimed to be through before church,
and he was, almost: unconscious
as a stone by noon, but
his dawdling heart kept
beating till half past five.

Cowboy Death

In those fifties TV shoot-em-ups
it always came to this: catch a bullet,
stiffen, grimace, die. No writhing, no
revolting gore, just instant, painless death.
So when I, callow Southern Baptist boy,
deigned to help our skeletal dying cow
from her pain into cow heaven,
I knew one well-placed twenty-two
between her eyes would work my gift.
But the skulls of large mammals are
(I learned by trial and error) very thick.
After four sharp cracks, she tightened
into one long, drawn-out moan. Then
desperate for the end, I tried another
through her left eye, then the right.
Though blind and bleeding, she,
bless her heart, refused to die.
The entire box of bullets through,
she still survived in a crazy swoon
from my puny hornets' nest.
Fooled by killing's hyperbolic
length and depth, I ran home shaking
in disgust, yet in the quarter hour,
came back stern with larger caliber
to fix my mess's vast diameter
and cleanse away her pain, the both
of us redeemed by higher power.

Black Hole

Every county has had at least one:
the boy who broke through the ice
and drowned in the lake. But does
plural diminish his terrible fate?
Does tragedy's universality
lend triviality? Not on your life.
Even though somewhat like war
where death is a dime a dozen
the stark specificity of Jim
shot all generals off their dark horses
when that black hole took him.
Though I scarcely knew the kid
(several years younger and 2 towns over)
good sleep was scarce for weeks.

Yet most of that cow pond was shallow
but under his unlucky hole
where the creek bed was deep.
And all of that horror at 8!
Old, I've had a million close calls
on ice, in cars, motorcycles, in bars,
with lightning while hiking,
dead blackouts when drinking.
So who handles the reasons,
takes care of the rhymes?
And who in hell seconds your motion
of oops when it's time?

Sublimation

Straight to vapor, snow will often go.
It skips the shapeless liquid part
and zips straight to its heaven in the air.
Impatient, that is where you went,
my stillborn star. This foolish
treading water in this life
just must have seemed too far
and much too deep for you
to hang around for years and watch
substantial things you learned to love
turn dust and make you weep.
Still, I wish that you'd dropped by
and visited your mom and me.
For though all passes, there is much to see.

Crap Shoot

Look back upon the almost-was,
like Pickett's maybe-not-today-
but-thanks-for-asking Charge; or
Truman's going soft on Little Boy;
or Lincoln's nixing theater for cards:
those for-better-or-for-worse actions
aborted, scuttled, revised,
thought the better of,
the life you almost lived,
or lost.

Deep in our woods, we boys
discovered a boggy truck-sized hole
in the wet-weather creek's course
where the clay must have momentarily
forgotten to be impervious,
like a convict's surprising softness
as he courteously opens a door
for some fellow traveler down
the hardscrabble path toward murder.

So after a big rain, we thought
we just might swim some
in that darkish topaz pool
surrounded by the weeds.
Yet it had a snaky look to it,
a snaky feel, holes and roots
receding back into the bank's secrets,
so that even its exotic coolness
and the serendipity of its
being revealed only to us
were not enough to nudge
the near-about forward into history.

But there was the neighbor boy
who later arrived at the same fork
and took the road less traveled
that made all the difference—
for soon he hauled from the hole

his beseeching self, hung with
clinging fits of wrist-thick writhing,
vivid partners in his dance.
He passed before any luck arrived,
his poor choice come up snake eyes.

Venus and T

Not over the river and through the woods,
but through the woods and into the river,
too fast and too drunk to make the curve
were Venus and T, partners in crime
who raised hell and were high most of the time.
They just disappeared. Not even a sliver
of evidence to their whereabouts could
ever be found. Many theories were built
then torn down. Folks thought they'd run off or been killed,
then finally forgot. Both orphaned square pegs
in the river's round hole surely deserved
to be more than fish food and bone-and-tooth dregs.
Then 40 years later during the drought
what was hidden inside finally stuck out
of their coffin of fluidity.
But little was left of Venus and T.
Just the gold chain Venus wore round her neck
and the bracelet she'd given T for his arm.
But the Ford that they'd stolen was not quite a wreck.
Paint, seats, tires, a motor, it runs like a charm.

T-bone

The county agent helped me pick him out—
the calf with straightest back and deepest flank,
pure-bred, brick-shaped, the calf that sent Dad back
to the bank to buy this steer, hint and hanker
strong that this little Hereford named T-bone
might beat all other steers and win the state.
I put him in the lot beside our house
that had a shed with sawdust on the floor,
his feedbox in the corner, and fed him
twice a day: sweet feed, beet pulp, with salt
and mineral blocks inside his shed, played
with him like a dog, scratched his curly head,
fed him the finest bought alfalfa hay,
halter-broke the little guy, taught him to
stand with one leg plumb under each corner
of his blocky, meaty frame, trained him
to come to his clever name, which began
to chafe as this big pet grew closer to
September, when the fair would come to town
and I'd parade him in the livestock show
where T would win, then to the big state fair
where he'd win again, two more ribbons there.
I slept beside him that night in the barn,
but good sleep never really came. Next day
ole T-bone excelled at the auction, too.
By the pound is the way it is for steak.
Before he left I touched him in the pen.
Dwindling or either crashing down
is the way all of the sweetest stories end.

Hardhead

When you're small you tackle with your head.
This twin-eared missile always brought them down!
I'd aim and close my eyes, they'd hit the ground,
whistle would blow, shazam! the play was dead.
I hit hard Friday nights for thirty games—
my tackling head brought me a sort of fame.

But life after high school just slides downhill.
My mother says my hard head makes her ill.
I jump from one dumb job into the next.
"Don't stand around! Get off your phone! Don't text!"
The jobs are fun until the jobs are not.
I end up spending time here home a lot.
Three letter jackets hang there in the hall.
Now I don't even wear them to the mall.

Uncle Rush Speaks

The body can't release within
sweets sweeter than adrenaline.
—Fireball Roberts

It always was *my* drug of choice:

In Little League I loved the fast
foul ball smashing my catcher's mask.
At linebacker I craved the way my helmet
rang their bells. The buzz from sweet hard
hits surpassed good grass. And boxing was
the place where fury made my blood get up
tall enough to whip somebody's ass.

Cowboy on the college team, I loved
riding the biggest, baddest bulls.
A Texas drawl announced my name,
while soon or late I landed in
the jarring aphrodisiac of dust.
(Before or post eight seconds, folks,
all bull dismounts end in a fuss.)

Next, I discovered motocross: so fast
around those flying curvy spaces.
I broke my goddamn leg in seven places!

But best of all was Viet Nam—
I know it's hard to grasp—
but I adored those bullets
whizzing past. War was one big
flaming raging Six Flags ride.

But what I hate's this endless peace and quiet.
The grave lacks anything that's moving fast
beyond that last exquisite Claymore blast.

Allie's Elegy

The frazzled folks who lived across the street
I'd hoped would learn to pen their puppy up.
She'd play along the edges of the road
down which the cars explode.

Occasionally I'd drop an overt hint:
"She's precious; it would really be a shame
if some fool driver going way too fast
should hit her going past."

But no adult or clever child took heed
and put Allie inside their fenced backyard.
And when I'd see her cross their yard and stray,
I'd shoo her back each day.

I hatched a plan to steal her when I could
and gift her to my sister miles away,
but *when I could* that week just couldn't be:
My boss dumped work on me.

Then Friday morning when I was up first
I spied her bloody blemish on the street,
and rushed to find a shoebox and the hoe:
Soon off to school they'd go.

If death were not so long and wide and deep
I'd steal her back, and in our house I'd keep
her safe from cars and trucks and fools who place
babies in a lethal space.

Advice

Since you've asked me I must tell you
that this seems not such a good idea;
seems, in fact, much like the botched
euthanasia of the wild puppies
you could not catch or scare away;
ergo, those poorly-placed gut shots
with that vintage British .303 you'd
mail-ordered from Kleins, Chicago,
that came with armor-piercing ammo,
which, since puppies aren't composed
of steel, simply whisked their bowels
out the other side to hang, as they,
who'd barely just arrived, commenced
their other-worldly arias and tornadic
whirls, and gnawed intestines till
their fires burned mercifully out.
Orchestrating that chaos in the backyard
while Aunt Emily rested after surgery
was to me idiocy heaped on madness.
But I still love you, Brother, adjacent
fruit on our gnarled and withered tree.
And since you've asked, I'll say again,
this also seems no great idea to me.

Home from Afghanistan

Was always proud my Bill was a Marine.
In dress blues Bill could grace a magazine
cover, if handsome was their goal. His phone
they sent back with his other stuff has shown
a land like Mars: so different from our farm.
How could those men let my boy come to harm?
My God, I wish he'd never itched to roam.
Just pieces of my son have come back home
to Crawfordville. I feel like I'm in hell
this rainy night. They say Bill sort of fell
into a trap laid by the Taliban.
A month to go, then things just hit the fan.
Giving my country Bill's the hardest thing.
From every mountaintop let freedom ring.

Yardman

I'll bet if all the zigs and zags and round-and-rounds
stretched out, we'd learn he pushed that thing
around the world a dozen times. He always
spoke polite, tight-lipped patois, yet I imagine
the pushing forward and the cutting off assuaged
a rage I cannot fault him for. Our race had kept
his in a box so long that leveling off the world,
chopping things all off even, became a righteous
meditation. So he cut his yard, and ours, and scores
of others, striding, pushing, pulling with his superior
endurance, making the unequal even, for at least
a week, until the inequalities grew back.
Those last years, he was way too old,
the summers way too hot. Things beyond
the yards were finally leveling off, but he
kept pushing, sweating, till the day came
when he repeatedly continued cutting the same
flat patch, over and over, and someone
called those folks that take us all away.
Old and uneasy, now I too cut in the hot, jagged,
uneven incessancy and wonder like I think he did:
When will this unending foolishness cease?

Estate Sale

O nameless, smiling lady in those snapshots
that I stumbled on out back among the trash,
please forgive us for not knocking.
We've excessively filled your excessive absence
with our excessive desire for bargains.
Stick-on tags are all over your things.
(Some 50% off!) Crass Sherlocks,
we bend at the waist, examining detail,
lacking only giant, comic magnifying glasses.
For me, Mrs. Elephant-in-the-room,
my thin, brief remembrance of you is thick,
as we rummage through the relics of your life.
Strangest of all the strangeness, though,
is your anonymity in your own house—
the staff don't seem to even know your name.
If there is some invisible residue of you,
surely it is here, in this warm ambiance,
this comfortable, so-very-you parlor
that we all ardently disassemble
with our baseball bats of greed.
Strangely, a Hail Mary bubbles up
beneath my cheap faux-pallbearer lips
as I load your chairs and books into my truck.

On the Euthanasia of Dogs

Last night I dreamed a mechanical dog—
It could bark, beg, curl up in my lap,
do everything that you guys did
but die, and all we'd be out ever
would be just parts and labor
when it broke—it'd never
break our hearts. The part I
really hate about the real
is how all life leaked out
of your bright, glad-to-see-us eyes,
inevitable as gravity that pulls
the bounce right out of every
playful ball. What's worse,
my funny, furry family, who
loaned us laughs over the years
but called all debt due at the end
in one lump sum of grief,
your days that taught mortality
were seven times as brief.

Snakebit

It's not the only house in Texas with
a hex on it. Hell, if any house stands
long enough, luck frowns on it too. Because
most people don't move and all people die.
It's a lie to think one place is healthy
and another is not just because of
a blot on its survival record. There's
not a foot of ground that has dirt without
human dust or ashes as part of its soil.
Still, sometimes it seems some places just
gleam with the twinkle of bone and bad luck.
Yet everyone's life is seasoned with several
fucked up dark days. Truth is we all step
barefoot out into the dark. Right here in the hall
they found Auntie after four weeks. Then
the puddle of Auntie was no longer stiff.
And all that in the high heat of summer.
I'm glad my sweet aunt left me the house.
Yet after eight years I confess I still sniff.

The Drowned Man

Man looks a lot like
the world, but with wrinkles.
They are the pain of being man,
that storm. Hardly a ripple
can be seen on real water.
But the mind can drown a man,
the mind can hold its head under
longer than you can hold your breath.
Like that man, real, that we found
at the edge of the river.
Floating, he had the look
of an insomniac finally dozing.
Long gone before he left,
he was a familiar catastrophe,
a bottle always breaking or sinking.
The river just happened to be there.
His lungs had been filling for years.

Uncle Cried Uncle

He selflessly stepped out into the yard
by his favorite tree, that water oak,
to freeze himself in time and space
and not print himself forever on
a wall and ruin a room with a hole,
an indelible hell in the family home.
Always thoughtful, but the thoughts
were now no longer full. "I would like
to abscond while me, myself, and I
recognize ourselves, don't have to ask why.
You can't begrudge me that. I would
like to remember the man in the mirror,"
he joked, no joke. "I want to still be here
when I leave, want to know, you know,
the fellow who's brought in the sheaves
for the blessed in this house these years."
He was a very thoughtful man, but all
meaningful thoughts were leaking out.
He could see before long there would be
nothing there, nothing between those
sad blue-green eyes, so he put one there,
small, yet huge for all concerned,
just one, just once and for all.

Plague

Death came down
as if out of the trees
and said, "Can't breathe?
Humph, you always took
that for granted!" And
nothing changed but everything.
People stayed indoors,
and the loose became chaste,
and some of the chaste
loose. The stores ran
low and people went crazy,
but death still came,
gloomy as rain. Heat
finally arrived outside like
the heat that had come inside.
Springtime bloomed unhappy
as all who were left
were bereft. The dead
screamed to the living,
"I was, I was!" Eventually,
life came back out
like life does. Like
bees or the flies,
you can hear it buzz.

Ghosts

Ghosts are holes where folks you knew should be.
Their stoppage stops you exponentially.
For those you hate, death's really not so hard,
but the holes for those you love are large.
Their vacuum takes up acreage in your heart.
Subtraction, not addition, is the part
that disturbs most: ghosts are not things,
they're emptiness; cavities that sting.
All contact's gone, only your love remains.
They leave their haunting memories in our brains.
The silliest holiday is Halloween.
Its jest is revealed often in our teens
when someone dear has died. Gone is all fear—
no spooks. Ghost just means forever never here.

THE INFAMOUS

The Widow Recalls the Storm

Wife battering? Child abuse? No.
He did have quite a temper, though,
but I never saw him hit a living soul.
There *were*, however the continuing wars
with others via The Inanimate:

The Bob Barr for Congress sign, before which
late one night he screeched our tipsy Bronco to a halt,
extracted Barr's two-faced face from our neighbor's yard,
then smashed the baby kisser's yellow pine backbone
to smithereens. The wooden slivers in his palm
required my finest tweezer skills.

Then there was the big blue Samsonite, gift
from my first husband (whom I was,
at the time, addressing on the phone)
that he kicked so hard it bounced off 2 walls
and broke his jealous toe.

And today as I called from that Amoco on Main,
I flashed back years and saw him in that booth,
rushed and in a rage about his 4 lost quarters,
hitting with his hand's heel the culprit phone,
then damning and shitting and son-of-a-bitching
in pain, commencing to beat that pay phone
senseless with its own receiver, as
I slumped down in the Ford's front seat,
not knowing who he was.

Over the years, there was the windshield
broken with his fist, succeeded by assorted
panes and lamps and sheetrock walls,
and culminating with his heart.
Oh sure, he drank a lot, but I
never saw him unfairly fight a man,
or beat a child, except himself.
I never saw him hurt a single soul,
except his own.

Poolroom

As Big Bob Mote would always spin,
that poolroom may have in fact been
the last bastion of the rough customer
in this pastel-painted world.
So you knew what trouble you'd cause
packing your pussy in there
like a hand grenade. Timing
was real good or real bad,
depending on perspective, with both
past and present boyfriend simultaneous,
at opposite poles at that amped-up bar,
that ten thousand-volt battery, jump
cables just itching to flash, and you
ever the live wire, perfectly aware
of how your walk in those jeans would
erect and point the hairs in every
nose and ear in there towards storm.
As heads turned, the air got thick.
The consequent crack of ball on ball
marked lightning. Inevitably, the charged
bodies with the arrows in their pants
repelled, strongest as they faced.
That's when you yelled and spun
and slapped the whole barn into a bedlam
of bad, bad bewilderment. One
can read the papers for the what. The why
was all your balled-up fire within
reached down between those legs
and pulled the pin.

The Catcher in the Wry

Way back, got jerked from second base to catcher
because of little rich boy's shitty arm.
First day a foul tip hit me in the balls,
so rich boy's dad bought me a cup,
which rubbed a weeping blister on both legs.
Squat down, stand up, squat down, stand up,
so I ditched the cup and took my chances.
It's then I learned loving taking chances
to see those cocky fucks swing hard as hell
and still strike out. Up close and personal revenge
was always sweet, foul tips be damned.
Third strikes are what I lived for way back then.
I'd stick that last strike in their faces.
Like pissing in those rich boys' Cheerios.

Just like these hard years now, all up the ass
of a rich man's house, spraying Acme's poison
on the termites. I take my chances there, too,
sucking the fumes a poor man has to bear.
But sweet as the chance of a clean-up hitter's flop
is the soft underbelly of a rich man's house.
I'll risk cancer, rats, a copperhead's bite,
even that rabid coon that bit my throwing hand
and blessed me with twenty injections in the belly
for a few good shots at the privileged SOBs
who've had me squat or crawl for my whole life.
All folks are full of darkness—so am I,
so before I leave, sometimes I crack a pipe—
just a little hammer-tap here and there,
to leave a little gift for my superiors.
The sound at night my mind dreams up at dozing
is big man's golden toilet's flushing, and knowing
the filth that fills even the richest, luckiest man,
his trophy wife and spoiled and rotten kids,
swirls down and around, by God, but not away
into the sewer, least not until a plumber visits.
I'm always with my hammer and pipe wrench.
Sometimes for weeks they can't locate the stench.
Their stink is proof the rich are full of shit.

Real Churches

Dad or dog, the dead hover.
They make you what you are.
Whether God exists or not,
these are your creators: they
build your walls and dig your wells,
shape your fears, set fires
inside your hells. Cry uncle.
Cry Uncle Clyde, specifically, who
put his hairy hand upon your knee.
He floats before your face today—
a slimy black balloon. Cry Uncle Clyde
was there to shape your darker ways.

Or Dad, who, post his odd demise,
looks at you with his poker face
each time you open morning eyes.
The last words you spoke: *I wish
that you were dead!* And so next
dawn he died, the only blessed time
he did what he was told. He minded
like your best dog in the road,
all eyeballs and entrails you
piled inside the Jim Beam box,
you trailing gore across the road,
leaking from the box's little slot.
Dad or dog, the dead hover—
except in bars, the real churches.

Mrs. Sharkly's War

Somehow, they think I'm fair.
That I like them all equally
with some sort of saintly
educator equanimity, as if,
although we're ridiculed, disrespected,
we like it, for all teachers to them
possess, or are possessed by, some sort
of masochistic blandness that allows
us to enjoy abuse. But I am the trap
I lay for these pushy marauders.
The ones I hunt are fools,
spoiled, crass fools somewhat like
Donald Trump: rude, mean, ugly
in the way my mother used the term ugly
to denote sociopathic nastiness.
There are several in every class
that sorely chap my ass.
But hidden inside the proper
teacher self, one can wait
like a bandit behind a big boulder
the arrival of the young fool's stagecoach
so as to Robin Hood his rowdy wherewithal.
Here he comes now, the kid
I've hated since that first class.
His name's already on the yellow slip
I'll send him to his fate with.
And where I let him sit, and with whom.
My trap is set. Now just to wait
and lower the goddamn boom.

Cad

They're like sponges, my wives,
soaking up my bad like greasy
dishwater or fish blood sloshed
across the linoleum low points of life.
Before my dark appearance on her horizon,
this one was a paragon: in storms a rock,
a mother almost professional,
a teacher clicking off 180 perfectly
attended days like an atomic clock.
Then I washed up on her beach—
huge, wounded, and sad, some clumsy-cute
albatross begging for adoption,
insidiously vectoring in my horny heart
that highly contagious disease
beginning in the long tan legs, moving
up into the damp and dizzier regions
where insane and hyperbolic fevers throb,
directing the brain to drop
down to where the action is.
By the time it returns to its penthouse of reason
my manners have improved
but Eve is never quite the same.
I am the Bosco stirred in her pure milk,
the trash dumped in her clear deep well.
She should have had better sense,
as her mother repeats. Should have
taken the time to know me better.
Should have seen this barefooted boy
headed home after the thunderstorm,
stirring and splashing and messing things up,
making for the mama of the house a hard time.

Demolition

When Lennon died and Reagan lived
I took it as bad omen. Young,
pissed, full of righteous fire,
I orbited every grievance with
some version of my No Nukes
sign. The eighties were all
full of poems of mine that
would not fly. I drank too
much. I lost the farm. Our
marriage failed. Demolition,
not construction, was the job
for me. I made a symbol of it,
found it fun to tear
the damn place down.
My favorites were
the chimneys, unused, cold,
with me on fire. I'd start
at the top, armed with a chisel,
hammer, sledge. I'd take
them down the way
my luck was taking me,
in chunks of bricks and dust.
Take that! I'd show, not
tell, with every blow. Each
day I notified the world
of cold and hard: *Goddamn
turnabout's fair play!*

Day's End

for Tom

Drunk, Tom, you're a Rorschach blot
that calls to mind this traveling salesman
from Mobile, my buddy row Big Ray,
who peddled little steel bands, like hard,
almost microscopic wedding rings—
the smallest bearings in the clutches
of a nebulous apparatus I never understood
that made accessories for resisters
on cutters used in the depression industry.
And drinking in some Day's End lounge
after hard-fought deals on the roads
through forgettable Piedmont mill towns,
he would speak in a way about friction and wear,
about punishment and inevitable replacement
that would call down upon me all darkness
and despair, all the triumphant hopelessness
and gloom of my great aunt Mary,
Grande Dame of Doom, who, hooked
to her morphine pump like she was refueling,
enjoyed her death with a vengeance.
Transfixed and translucent while the black
of death and white of life changed places,
she pinned her sons for six slow months
like insects in the black and velvet shadowbox
of guilt with her twisted weapons of memory.

And so at day's end, this seedy gauche man,
empty as a drained and foamy stein,
held forth, and as he loudly gabbed,
Entropy, Death, Despair, those assassins
of Freedom, Truth, and Beauty as we know them
would gather round our booth we named John Wilkes
between the midnight-painted walls,
and desperately backed up against those walls,
I would have no recourse
but to drink it all to hell again.

And so it would begin again, the desire
to drown the unease, then celebrate the drowning,
to simply enjoy the floating back and forth
through the jolly voices to the john, resplendent
in the painless tickly fuzziness of beer. But
always at that point in the lubricated evening,
happy in the higher regions, free
of Aunt Mary, yet still cautious,
I'd begin careful instructions to myself
on the finer points of staying to the right
of all the centerlines, however myriad.
The early morning's motto is *Alert, but casual.*
Simply a case of remembering who one is,
and where, an instance of collecting more than
half one's wits and errant movements, the trick
of getting into the right car and into drive,
that good ole gear programmed for home.

But home directly, Tom, is not always possible,
as we have, with the ample aid of Atlanta's Finest,
scientifically proven, replicating our results four times.
Tom, fellow bard, Poet Laureate of Milwaukee,
let us call it the dislocation of good sense,
the unwilling suspension of the poet's license.
Disbelief, Thomas. Let us call it
drunk and disorderly disbelief, like
later being told one pissed in one's shoe.
Just another last time, Tombo.
Let us call it time to quit.

Jackoff of All Trades

Those Mexicans always replace a roof
in half the time that me and Johnny can.
I've heard they can live fifteen to a house
or trailer that they stay in in some park.
They look like spiders crawling on a roof,
tearing the old one off in half a day,
then by dark the new one's nailed in place.
We can't compete with that, just me and John.
It takes us both at best at least a week.
Both him and me, we hated junior high,
so we just up and quit in seventh grade.
And Parker Johnson let us help his crew.
That's where we learned to strip and nail a roof
and frame a house and hang and finish rock.
You want it done, ole John and me can do
most anything. Still, there's only two
of us and we are getting old. Then out
of nowhere come these folks who live on
only air. I swear I thought that we was poor,
but these folks live like natural beasts.
They work like hell and work for less and still
they send some wages back to Mexico.
They steal your job and work from dawn to dusk.
But worse is that they make me feel so slow.

News Flash

Two dead in murder/suicide,
it said. Two more I did not
know, and never will. Unless
some heaven waits far out
there still. Yet there's no word
from those I've known.
What's gone is gone, from
all I've seen or heard. The
graveyard is the most inert
place on earth. Even
the breeze there makes
no haste. So I can't help but
wonder why one of said two
would try so hard to race
beyond this tasty pie
of animation. The hearse
the husband chose has no
reverse, and postal service
sucks from that null nation.

Like A Good Neighbor

Jane, let's get together, grab a bite
then I can hang your back door before night.
I'm sorry Bob has been ill all these years.
I know his poor health's caused you both some tears.

Now that you've both moved twenty miles away,
it's great to see you back again today
to cut the lawn and rake up all these leaves.
You look great in that red blouse without sleeves

and those tight shorts. I hope the old house sells,
but not too soon. I walked across the street to tell
you that I'm here to help you if I can.
Heavy stuff sometimes requires a man.

Catherine's at work from 8 to 6 each day.
While she's at work this rat can work or play.

Guilt

In September's dusty heat
the young folks came
with their quart fruit jars
to our back spigot for water,
first asking Miss Cora Mae's
permission, then heading back out,
all business, to their cotton sacks
left in the great puzzle-piece
fields of endless brown
shot through with fluffy white stains.

In fourth grade, just off the bus from
school, on our new Zenith in the den
I'd be watching Officer Don
of the ridiculous *Popeye Club,*
who, seemingly confused
and against all better judgment,
frequently jammed his hand
into the ooey-gooey bag filled
with broken eggs and mud
and chocolate syrup, to the delight
of the giggling peanut gallery—

but oddly I would make a point
to be out of sight when the dark,
unbathed, un-*Leave-It-To-Beaver*-ish
children from the fields walked
to our house. (How different
our town was from those
Main Streets on TV.)

Something uncomfortable and dark
gnawed at the wiring in the attic
of my head while those children,
excused from their school to pick
our crops, knelt beneath azaleas

in our yard to fill their jars with flat
warm well water from our garden hose.

And yet, distracted by the antics on
our set, I feasted on my milk and Oreos.

The Baby Speaks

Yeah, he's my brother, but my love for him
is seasoned with a salty pinch of hate.
Too long I had to strain over, around,
or through his thicket of trophies to find
a spot to sun my pasty hide unshaded by
the tower of his sporty deeds. All-State
in basket, foot, and base, his giant balls
dwarfed mine. And if that weren't enough,
he took my measly G.P.A. and doubled it
to 4. Around the supper table I was wanted,
dead or alive, for smallness, stupidity,
and sloth. Bound tightly by relentless
sibling love, I often roared awake to war
with him to squeeze a tiny ego's space
in which to breathe. Today, Mom says, since
I've *finally* found my way, that Tim and I
equate a matching pair. I will admit
she may be right, now that we've got beyond
the poison of the fighting all those years.
The proof that we're strange xeroxed twins burned
stark back in our tiny room of tall and short
in that one mirror of our contested space:
The striking bare similitude
of my dumb ass and his exalted face.

Sorcerer's Rope

after Andrew Hudgins

"See that old rope hanging down from that limb?
Let's say it's a sorcerer's rope," said John,
my coworker from the mill.
"Let's say if you tugged it, there'd be
a brilliant flash, and asshole Freddy,
our infamous supervisor-from-hell
would instantaneously disappear.
Would you pull it?"

"The man's got a family, John. Wife,
3 kids, and a baby on the way."

He snapped his fingers hard. "Shazam!
I'd delete that rascal from the earth.
There's welfare and she'd find a decent guy.
I've heard he beats her too.
The things the jerk has put us through.
I'd pull it in a heartbeat—poof!
I'd cut that bully and his meanness loose."

"Old Fred's had a hard life.
I've heard his dad would whip him,
lock him supperless in the basement."

"Don't care how the bastard came about;
Just want him gone—I want relief.
Think I'd kill him if I had the chance."

As we stared at the rope, it swayed
in the hard breeze like a noose.

Somewhere in Sunday School, a boy,
learning about turning the other cheek,
thinks, "Uh-uh!"

Mob

Look, a crowd of kindred souls
has gathered for this push-and-pull
to lift itself upon its golden
pedestal of pomp and bull.
"We're good," they roar, "you're bad!"
through hyperbolic bullish horns.
"We're right, you're wrong!"
repeats this kick-ass wound-up throng.
Sometimes one hellion is a crowd,
but worse is when a mob blends one.
With three's-a-crowd times hundreds,
nice folks transform to hellions.
This mob stomps staunchly stern.
(Amusing, seen from roofs.)
They're too smart for their good,
yet show strong primate proof:
Crowds exhibit all the signs
of crass chimpanzee-hood.
The mob begins to gyre,
pirouettes to hurricane:
angry clichéd placards thrust—
their word-spears lust for pain.
All this tornadic raging heat,
once known for torches, tar,
feathers, nooses, grief.
Sure of history's mommy smile,
this solid legion's now thick and stiff.
Whether lemmings or God-damned swine,
this suicide of fools runs off my cliff.

Slow Learner

Fifteen years before he learned he drank
too much, he'd gotten drunk again,
and when the bar closed, headed home
down curvy River Road. Then city slicker,
five years post farm, oblivious ex-slave
to weather that so long held his daddy hostage,
he forgot the past week's passel
of hard spring rain, and, upon seeing
the giant sawhorse, exclaimed,"Shitfire!"
and floored the GTO, selecting the middle
of the striped barrier to smash,
to part it like the Red damn Sea,
refusing some silly detour's delay,
for he needed to get home and pee.
Next thing he knew he was cutting spray
and then sailing his boat the floating car,
then in Clarke County jail, piss can in the corner.
Thus, his impatient bladder got its wish.
Sobriety, however,
had to wait a decade and a half.

Bad Boss Confidential

My outer skin is smooth;
my inner surface cratered
like the moon. Those early wounds
hide deep inside my smile.
Self-worth, that plastic elf
upon my closet's bottom shelf
powers all my fiery prayers
aimed crooked by my fears.
Most times my anger cheers
someone's dire fate. Too late,
or not at all comes empathy.
King of my hell, if I were
not so small, mercy might reign
inside my wounded heart and brain.
The hurt that I received
ballasts any trace of sweetness
that might rise up to light.
Poor Jesus chose His cross;
Mine came unbidden
and it made me mean.
Relief comes only when
I wish for others' pain.
What damns my soul
appears to raise me up.
I cruise around this
warehouse in spite's truck.

Wednesday, When I Called

When I look two wives back
I see now she always was
one husband short. The one
there now is five feet four
and gone five days a week.
In his truck, that phone book
he sits atop has myriad
numbers written in his hand.
Hell, the old gal's girlish leg
was snakebit from the start.
So Wednesday when I called
to try again to make amends,
she, softer than expected,
softened me enough to see
the sorry vacuum of my years—
throughout which, round
and round, I chased my tail,
and others', too. At last, almost
in charge, I hope I've finally
fired myself from foolery,
leaving the mirror in my locker
for the next narcissist. Luke-
warm father, piss-poor spouse,
don't get me wrong, I chose
to have my cake and eat it, too.
Yet I do regret while screwing,
strewing sad, delicious chaos all
around, I didn't, like Larkin, strew
among my stacks of naught
a few more decent poems.

Murder House

I've seen the TV ghost hunters do it:
find the infamous home or madhouse dorm
or ancient prison cell from hell, and sit
and claim tormented human souls ooze out
like spores from toxic mold to nauseate,
chill the air, and terrorize the hunters there.
But here, in spite of all I know about
this house, I'm like an ant in Lincoln's skull—
the walls are there, but all equipment's gone.
And all it sees is hard insensate bone
surrounding air and dust and muted light.
I'm ashamed to say that I almost go
to sleep. The only ghosts I feel are those
of trees split into planks, and freest earth
squeezed into walls of hard, plumb plaster board.
In here I'm pretty sure the deaths have died
and dumbly rest in peace. We're dust to dust;
our torment lies between. In peaceful gilded
autumn light these mindless dust motes mill.
They drift like tiny carefree bloodless sheep
through golden hills of inorganic air.
They gambol down then swirl back up again,
just like they did that sunny murder day.
Dust is dying's meekest circumstance.
Old loss of blood is moot to mindless trance.

Anatomy Lesson

She said that she had turned eighteen last May.
Otherwise, I'd never looked her way.
She stood out from the sophomores in my class.
Unfortunately, quite a piece of ass.

Sometimes she'd visit my lab after math.
She'd talk of risqué stuff like taking baths.
I know I'm married, but I couldn't stop.
One afternoon, Lacy removed her top

and that was that. From there both balls rolled down
her hill. My whole damn world spun round.
I took that three-month roller coaster ride,
but lost wife, kids, the job, and all my pride.

Today I'll humbly plead before the court:
If jailed, I cannot pay my child support.

Niches

Funny how people and mice
live in the same house
but not in the same spaces.
Floyd Street with the Baptist Church
and the brothel nearly next door—
same neighborhood, different niches.
"One for the ladies, one for
the bitches," said Uncle Bob,
who was no snob, with his plug
of Red Man and his galluses
that held up his dirty Dickies.
But Uncle Luke was, with his
masters and PhD. "Oh my!"
Bob would mock, concerning
his brother, the finicky bachelor
and his oh-so-proper ways.
And the blacks in town
during those Jim Crow days
in the same town as us
but at the back of the bus,
so to speak. No water fountains
for them and no movies, either,
except in the balcony up
those shaky old stairs in the back
of the Strand. Oh, what a time
it was to be white, say many
Caucasians today. The gray
concrete rebel still rides high
on his steed on the square, cheered
toward battle by mums and begonias
in his vertical, anachronistic
tube of 19th century air,
this zeitgeist's rathole there.

Squirrel Creek Farm

The pecans and the oaks twitched round the place:
Scads of squirrels zoomed through arboreal space.
The acorns and the pecans fed them well,
but fear of fire sent myriad squirrels to hell.
Chewed wires in the attic sealed their fate—
both brothers honed their fear into a hate
that necessitated gunplay in their heads.
They filled up umpteen buckets with the dead
and dumped those once-quick critters in the creek.
(Perhaps the sin's not eating hunted meat.)
That creek was worried red by gunfire's mess,
but what flowed down came back around, I guess:
Just next year, incessant spring rains flooded.
Squirrel Creek swelled, unleashed its repressed id
and swept that hot-wired house clean off its piers.
(I see it float and burn across the years.)
Their mother trapped inside was never found.
Somehow a crazy narrative got round—
some storied, country foolishness, enhanced—
that on its flaming gable, gray squirrels danced.
Both brothers ended in the Asian war.
I guess blood sticks its foot inside death's door.

Killer

When I got home from Desert Storm
the crazy terror hit me like a bomb.
My stress was caused by nothing—
all the nothing here back home—
smiles and laughter, calm drove me
to drink. Then County Chairman Johnson
hoisted a few with me, we talked,
he said he had a job he thought
might fit me to a T, to tie some
loose ends up. He chuckled, then
called my job Euthanatologist,
and said I'd have a truck, new
Remington, free cartridges, good pay.
He said just be available each day—
Sunday too, to make "house calls"
to where a deer's been hit, stray
dogs after a calf, maybe wild hogs.
It calms me down to see them die,
I don't know why. Guess red's
my favorite color. Even after all
these years my aim's as steady
as it was when I cleared out those
black-haired fellows on the other side.
My heart's a happy hammer when I kill.
Hey, you got a mess to fix, I will.

Mr. Cutter of The Sandtown Group

We sealed the deal today.
Bought 300 acres, J.T. Smith's old farm,
grown back now: all mature timber,
from his grandson in Atlanta.
Huge pines, hickory, poplar, oak,
acquired before the damned tree huggers
could find a way to kill our deal,
declare some goddamn critter there
endangered. They turn what's left
of my thin hair to gray! Anyway,
the only useful thing that forest does
is grow some big-racked bucks to shoot!

Tonight, we partners celebrate:
good whiskey, prime rib, rare steaks,
then estimate the monumental haul
we'll make clearcutting our new land.
I hate the moonscape of stumps and tops
and red ruts left by hard spring rains,
but you have to wait a year or two,
or sometimes three, till the time is sweet
to build a mall or sell to one who will,
or a company hot to build a factory.
Ultimately, you see, you have to
choose your favorite shade of green:
Touchy-feely chartreuse for the birds,
or the sweet army green of money.

The Landlord Discusses Business with His Son

It's time we kick them out of number 9.
Delay will only magnify our loss.
The key to good eviction is conviction:
You've got to let those fuckers know who's boss.

It's, too, I think, past time to raise the rents.
Inflation eats at profit all the time.
And don't forget that too much mercy hurts:
It costs big when we listen to their whines.

And for God's sake don't mention asbestos.
It's harmless if you never stir it up.
Word gets out and our asses would be toast.
Environmental claims always blow up.

Most times it's best to let sleeping dogs lie.
To sum up, keep costs low and all rents high.

Boomer at the Birth of Jim Crow's Doom

80 million people died,
then we were born.
Our four-square parents believed
the world was cured.
Smiling, they pointed upward
as our flag climbed to the top.
We had a farm with white face
cows, and grew cotton, too,
bright white in a dark tangle.
Daddy kept some folks he
called primitives to tend it.
Church, where we learned to be good—
right from wrong being important—
was poorly understood. At each very
white xmas, we sang along
with vinyl Bing at chapel
at our pale narrow school.
Strangely, we all slept well at night.
In our dark, even with the windows up,
we never heard the drastic train coming,
delivering God from the opposite direction.

Pale William's Lament

Neatsfoot oil and old foot sweat
from hundreds of holey pairs
waiting for their owners to return
gave Bill's Shoe Shop, to say
the least, a unique atmosphere.
But your favorite shoes made new
with a two-buck half sole and a heel
was a steal. And Big Bill's Grill
was the tasty place to eat, long
before McDonald's came to town.
Oh I miss the way things were:
Folks stayed in their places. And Bills
like me were everywhere, not Juans,
not Hakeems.
               Hell, I cut my baby teeth
on Buffalo Bill, Wild Bill Hickok,
the notorious Billy the Kid, then
later at Jasper High, they threw in
some Bill Shakespeare for the sissies.
Long after the Northern aggression,
when both the world wars flared,
Bills wore the white hats.
Billy near single-handedly won
the goddamn things, with the help
of a Bob and a Dick and a Tom.
Then America was great. Even
Aunt Daisy's favorite flower was
Sweet William, back when schools
were black or white, not black
and white. Now all might of
white is fading. Now we Bills
are all out of shells, desperate
behind a dead horse at Little Bighorn.

Pale William as a Boy

So much of the future
was about that red tractor,
the red tractor that he couldn't
drive and nobody would
offer to teach him. Hell,
he might get hurt on that
red tractor, so the shiny
strong-smelling machine was
left to their sharecropper, or
even his son who was younger
than Bill: the little impotent,
spoiled, delicate white boy.
And soon it was clear they were
faster than him, could jump
higher, sing better, and he heard
were even slicker with the girls
than little weak blond waifs.
Odd ain't it, how he turned
his world upside down and
made the bottom the top
and hated them for all
they could do and he couldn't?

THE EXHAUSTED

Cobbler

What would a cobbler say,
ill-suited as he is to this age,
to our baby bartender here?
Struck dumb, I am that cobbler,
or maybe a cooper, or collier—
whatever in hell that is. Heck,
the times have changed, right
under my anachronistic nose.
Buildings are taller, liquor
stronger, girls prettier, but
distant as Mars. The damn
weather itself races only forward,
not marching in place like when
we were boys. Sure, back then
there were arrows on the ends
of time, but time had a mild,
round blankness to it, almost
like a face on which you could
paint a sort of smile, making
the universe gruff but friendly,
because we were made mostly
of future. And when we spied
old men, the silly smiles we
painted on the world looked
back at us from them: They
looked at us, amused, and joked,
and we looked back at them,
amused, nodded our heads
respectfully, and smiled. Then
I thought the eyes of the old men
looked wisely at this world,
easy eyes—nothing like ours now:
scared, and vigilant for death.

Voice from the Window Bed

Shrinking here in room 308,
I'm excited by this sharp light
as I have finally in the merciless, blazing
window to my left witnessed the pure
substance and shadow of screen wire.
I've had a long, star-crossed tryst with it,
the way it stretched around my life,
strained from stagnant air the very flies,
yet kept me in, there where it stretched, bellowed,
gained dimension on the backdoor where I stayed.
And screen too on my selfish eyes, the windows
of my stubborn head, my house of pride.
The long noses of loved ones touching my life
asked so much of me I left home for good.
Now hard absence touches this old residue.

Once in youth, (that dream almost forgotten)
not to hurt Papa in the sweetness of his gift,
I pulled thin wires from our screen door
to make my stringless second-hand fiddle sing.
But my long jig is almost finally up.
And always, even though always has been
interminable, tight net has covered me
like scales on the eyes of us trapped in the Bible.
And my body, this finely constructed animal cage
that God could free me from but won't,
I don't know why. Hell, all screen is
is a zillion tiny crosses welded together
that will surely work like some holy sin filter
to sieve out my damned meanness.

So like Miss Etta Clay of the adjacent
and now-empty bed, I must try and try
and try to stretch myself thin and translucent
over my screaming bones, harden and point
my soul to dive beneath the flesh
like some precious but deadly cold needle,
squeeze beneath these bars and wheels and tubes
and break my 83 Sisyphean years

of rage and uselessness into atoms small
enough to pass through screen
and out of slavery from myself for my self,
like pollen from some nameless, blameless tree.

Old Jock at Sunny Shores

When forced by time to punt, this golden
coast is where we dropped back to,
to quit the game, drop out of the race,
circle the wagons for our last frail stand.
Fore! Those of us who can still swing
plink hard these balls in your baby faces,
for we're bitter that our time of prime
has passed. Our carts zip spryly as dancing
white shoes over these cheery green hills,
yet there are traps on this sturdy chartreuse:
sunken dunes and slimy hazards of malignancy,
clots and blockages leering at us along
these manicured paths of geriatric glee. This
sunny-faced meadow is no graveyard, quite,
but we do whistle our way one way through
its shag carpeted rough, for we're old,
almost-cold squares from the Roosevelt Era.
Fairview's this place I chase my balls;
Lawnwood's next door where soon we'll
all learn gardening from the bottom up.
Yeah, I'm bitter; bitter, yet grateful—
for today I've made it to the eighteenth
again under the blue sky, still standing
on serviceable legs, pain-free, and so happy
it damn near doubles this no-longer-cool cat's
shrill, insatiable, all-but-forgotten ninth life.

The Ladies

When Mom and Mae got old
and both their men were dead
we moved the pair in Mom's house,
split the rambling maze of halls
and rooms into a sort of duplex,
dead-ending halls into closets,
cutting doors in walls, dividing
the place into two halves, separate,
but equal, right down the middle,
so each sweet lady would have her
privacy. We prided ourselves in
knowing that *our* splitting of the races
was actually equitable, each side
with nearly the same square footage,
each with its own same-size bedroom
and identical bath, complete with sink,
toilet, tub, just different colors—
one pink, one green. Each duplex
even had its own T.V. room, the kitchen
being their only common space.
Yet after all the pricy remodeling,
the opening of this and closing of that,
every day when I'd visit after work I'd find
the retired clerk and her former maid
in Mom's den in side-by-side recliners,
the old bluebird and the cardinal
washed colorless as sparrows by the soaps.

Ghost Hunter

As if on a midnight
tour of infamous homes
I watch the silly TV
ghost hunts laden with
the fulsome tools and gauges
of pseudoscience, but all
I really see are the
flash-lit faces of fools
channeling Warhol.
Yet I know what a ghost
is; I know the terror. She
is the loved-one-shaped space
where my dear was,
her loveless absence.
That's the ice, the chill
running down my spine,
it's her vacuum in my now,
not some sheet-covered hooha
intruding on life.
Heat always flows
from hot to cold
and plunges from your heart
into the void. Ghost
means gone.
The only presence
moving through this emptiness
is me.

Our Dying Neighbor Cuts the Grass

Was it my own misanthropic warp
that made him annoyingly epic?
(I've always hated big, long-winded things.)
Or was it my childish denial of the truth
of every life's inevitable closure?
(I should love you all, at least a little,
knowing fate.) Now he looks so thin,
so small and brief, there on his new
Green Machine, Procrusteanizing
the poor grass, taking out his prognosis
on its pouring forth of perpetual verdure.
The grass's height is the last thing
under his control, as he back-and-forths
toward the vanishing point. Death
in suburbia strikes like a bell, or
lightning, juxtaposed as it is against
such manicured perpetuity. Here
recently we've lost three dogs,
four cats, two of the elderly, even
a suicide who bled out upon his
patio's terra cotta tiles—yet
nothing on the outside changes,
everything stays green and clean,
ironic as a neighbor's smile.

High Blood

Last week he killed Rick's beagle
with a hot dog soaked in antifreeze.
Which stopped the all-night barking
but knocked the scab off years
of ire between the two.
The situation's risen to a head—
seems not unlikely more besides
old Ace may end up dead.
Ace was Rick's sweet soul, but
all sweetness morphed to rock and roll.
No eggheads here on Pissed-off Street—
just four scarred, calloused hands,
two old muddy pickup trucks,
and jacket-pocket Glocks.
The long guns in both houses
stand erect as sex in corners.
I wouldn't be surprised if Pabst
Blue Ribbon helps both men
keep the scared eye open
while the tired eye sleeps.
And every time the door knocks
the heart of each man leaps.

At Woodlawn

What a crowd turns up here,
supine beneath this jungle of turf,
shining from these clean stones.
Still, I'm feeling somehow they see
the same blinding blue as me
where heaven once was. All this reputed
repose should comfort, I suppose,
but looking down I'm stopped dead
by dirt. Yet I'll bet when they turn
and sneak a peek down death's abyss
it's like when I survey the top of this pine,
then refocus higher to circling crows,
and again further up to the silver jet.
For surely there's subverted sky in death,
inverted, with deeper niches for profounder
rank; And the hooks of the dead, too,
spectrumed from shallow to deep, wishing
that something, as promised, would bite.
Surely that's what all this silent, still
waiting's about. Some type of fishing.

Hard Time

The cancer showed up
like a cat creeping into the yard.
By that I mean no fanfare,
no hoopla, maybe a breeze's
ruffling of leaves, or cold
moonlight. No bells ringing, no
whistles blowing. Just another
every other, till the diagnosis
came with that little odd
pain. Then things changed,
mostly inside, where the fear
roared class 5 hurricane.
Everything outside that hell
looked pretty much the same—
yet not quite: At once, trees
loomed taller, boulders bigger,
holes deeper. Roads much longer—
everything in the world got farther
apart. I wasn't so smart anymore,
either. My future tall thirty
guaranteed years of good luck
now had hexes on them.
Was there nothing I could keep?
Pain has a trash can lid it bangs,
so you can't sleep. And fear,
that little boy blue, blows his
damn horn all night, too.
Wide awake in the gloomy house
you can feel death—fat, still, dark—
intent on you, the mouse.

The Old Man and the Black Dog

The night was cold and the window was up.
The old man and the black dog
would curl up together on the bed
under an old sleeping bag. Now the man
no longer worked, he and the dog spent
all of their time together. They took
long walks, and the dog would ride
everywhere in the cab of the man's truck.
He was protective of the old man,
and the old man was protective of him.
The man worried about living longer
than the dog and often tried to figure
how many years the dog and he might have.
He was glad he was old, that what remained
might match the dog's exponentially fast years,
for the dog would be sad without him
and he would be sad without the dog.
One night in a dream, the old man's youth
was offered to him all over again by God.
The man asked God if he would
make a special exception for the dog
so he would age at the same rate people do.
God said He couldn't go that far with his goodness.
The old man thanked God, but said he'd have
to decline the offered youth. He thought
God smiled a little just before he drifted back
into dreamless sleep. When he woke in the dark
the dog was licking his face. Both got up,
went out back and peed in the dark yard.
And because there was nothing to be done,
the two fell back into deep sleep and slept late.

Mirror, Mirror

You backwards old dyslexic,
we're lucky this razor's not straight.
Do you sometimes feel dizzy, too,
meeting me coming and going?
Daft handy man, fix thy own self
with your cattycornered jokes
and tall-tale tools: your left-
handed monkey wrench and
ridiculous board stretcher—
stretch this spent life out!
You lighter-than-air old fart,
your hot air is stale, short breath:
COPD: corny old people die:
a truth that's strongest when
the fear is larger than the light.
Cracked visage, while you float
in air, walking in my shoes
is something you can never do.
Still, we're tied tiredly together.
I sweep house dust out with the dirt,
my back, my knees, my ankles hurt.
I'm damned sure that it won't be long—
I'll be that dust and you'll be gone.

Fourth Step

God seemed a bit Jerry Falwell: too fat,
a stern blowhard to dread. But old Bill's term,
higher power: not bossy, quasi-detached, instead,
the difference the distance between, say,
Dick Nixon and Mohandas K. Gandhi, or some
rusty ancient claw hammer and a red begonia.
It's hard to explain, but maybe the drinking
softened me up, as well. All those overly
saturated years of hell will, you know.
I think after all that, the top, the bottom,
all four sides, and the ends were ready
to blow. Yet I really hated surrender,
to confess my sins to numerous folks.
It got my goat to admit to being a heel.
But the weight that admission relieved
floated hell straight up into heaven.
Owning up brought me fish, supplied loaves.
But my new higher power provided
the Zebco, the hook, and the leaven.

Preserves

Memory crushes those lucky with longevity.
Death's density accumulates in every old life.
The depth of all that accrued strife is over
its owner's head, and his or her heart
clogs with tombstone limestone,
for all the old bear internal cemeteries:
Cut us open for crosses, cherubs,
obelisks, pale angels of stone.
The point that deserves attention
is the point of great attrition—
when the dear dead exceed the living.
Their mere volume bends the back bent.
For years there was the dribble,
the slow drizzle of disappearance,
but then, or so it certainly seems,
the bottom drops out and dying becomes
irresistible fad, mandatory algorithm,
and one's loved ones and cohorts fall,
fail in this futile battle to stay on top
of the earth. The crumbling dearth of those
remaining exceeds anyone's explaining.
Humor turns gallows, or disappears.
Fears increase. No wonder folks lose hope.
Yet conversion can perform inversion.
Then anxiety often loosens
into resigned relaxation, a kind
of settling deep down in one's chair
when what is there seems greater
than what's here. Most faces that you
see in dreams are faces of the dead,
for death seems really not the best
word for where they are.
Somehow in sweet fatigue you may
see them on some star, far away
and dream there'll be no more
harsh heaviness that scars.
Inverted, the past seems future
as down into the cellar you will go.
Her peaches! You strain and twist
the top off Mom's old jar.

Subtraction

At first you could be anything:
president, baseball star, a great writer.
But subtraction adds up over the years.
Then what you can be
becomes less and less,
the fire in the man
burning lower and lower,
the speed of its light
slower and slower.
Even the time left
dwindles anxiously in the joy
or thankfully in the pain,
and finally you soak
broken-hip-deep in the nursing home,
losing into the stark soup
even the letters of your name.

Mac Gay was born and raised on a 280 acre farm near Newborn, Georgia. He stumbled across contemporary poetry in his mid-twenties and was immediately hooked. Before the discovery occurred, he had already earned two degrees in the sciences at the University of Georgia. Later he obtained another degree in creative writing from Georgia State University. He is the author of 2 other full-length poetry collections: *Ghost Hunt*, runner-up for Eyewear Publishing's 2017 Beverly Prize and *Our Fatherlessness* (The Orchard Street Press, 2021) as well as 4 chapbooks. His chapbook *Farm Alarm* was runner-up for Texas Review Press's 2018 Robert Phillips Poetry Chapbook Prize and *Physical Science* won Poems & Plays' 2003 Tennessee Poetry Chapbook Prize. His work has been anthologized in *The Southern Poetry Anthology: Georgia* from Texas Review Press and his poems have appeared in numerous magazines including *Atlanta Review, Crosswinds, Cutbank,* and *The American Journal of Poetry.* A longtime runner, biker, and hiker, he lives with his wife Jana, their 2 dogs and 4 cats in Covington, Georgia and teaches English at Perimeter College of Georgia State University.

CPSIA information can be obtained
at www.ICGtesting.com
Printed in the USA
LVHW010239260722
724372LV00005B/241

9 781604 542660